Poem

SPRING

A CHAPBOOK OF POEMS
BY STEPHEN M. FORRESTER

A gift of original works

To Ulana.

Like stars to the heavens, you guide me. Always.

"As the crows hark, let the sparrows rest.
Be happy."

-S M. Forrester

Poems For
SPRING

Tailored Rays

Be you the heavens' tailored rays,
Thor's wind and Zeus' wrath,
Of light's light and long lost,
I'd call upon and guide you:
But you being sun have only your arms,
Your warming hand and nectar.
Take your might and guide me.
For I, like the weather,
Now my heart will melt with the snow.

The Calling

Wings flutter like fire.
Colours, radiate and bloom.
Calling, in spring's noon

The Sun, The Morning, And The Crow

The glow will shine, the greens will wave;
The whistling of grass in the lands.
The smile has opened as the morning yawns,
And the fields, they dance as they grow.

The wind holds softly a butterflies embrace.
The wasps will hover and flow.
"Come with me", said a smile upon the land.
The sun, the morning, and the crow.

A Morning Call

Could you dance with the jester of calling tones,
Lost in chain of a wheel?
Of on and on, of a robin's call,
Or a sparrows hark in a veil?

Their song, like a crooked man.
Their hail, jolly in kind.
As the birds shall call for their wanting,
You wake, weary listener,
Weary waker, to a vow.

The Frost Now Sleeps

Had foresight won the glorious blaze,
Took hold the sombre might, of dusk,
Of God's fright and night's night,
Of all the valleys of Eden's sight,
You could carry your shadow,
And venture on your waking days:
But you, just a humble cold,
You snuggly let your blankets flare.
Not open, but to dust;
The frost now sleeps.
The frost, now gone and soundly.

The Fox In The Roses

As the waking moon calls to the fox in the roses,
Did you open up your hand?
Did you wonder?
Did you cry?

As the waking moon calls to the fox in the roses,
Did you smile, or did you belay?
The heat rises as the dawn calls,
And the people wink another day.

As a waking moon calls.
As a waking moon calls.

As the waking moon calls to the fox in the roses,
In the kiss of starlight's May,
A single petal falls in wind,
And a heart now grows in the bay.

Wall Of Light

"Breakthrough," the mountains called,
With the butterflies, the daffodils, and the breeze.
"Breakthrough," harked the angels,
As darkness slept,
And the air hugged the bunnies and the bees.

The time had come for colours call,
And iridescence filled and glowed.
The wall of worlds and greens, reborn.
The wall of light, now grow.

Spring's Wind

Messages don't tire.
Whisked in wings of all colour,
Winds, serene with sun.

Can You Hear?

Whistle.

Whistle.

Whistle. Can you hear?

Just like life is born from the water,
Pollen now flies like the sands.

Loves Longing Light

If the feathers encompassed light's righteous hand,
Adorned by the beauty of tales,
Wrought with the air,
And the colours of flowers, loves longing light,
And dew drops of crystal that fall from the air,
I'd sleep for a day, and sleep for another.
I'd reach in eternity and embrace restful fate.
The calming smoke that surrounds my beating,
So peaceful, my heart:
Had the heavens encrusted a pillow of dreams,
Had I lay in the purity of light.
But the peace and serenity could never compare,
To your warming hands, day and night.

Flight Of The Rainbow

Were you pointing at heaven?
Were you pointing at me?
Were you pointing to the leprechaun,
Cantankerous and green?
The butchers, and bakers,
The frogs and the flies,
The treasure of rebirth,
The plants that survive?
You were born of the water,
Now you conquer the skies.
Not in flight, like a butterfly,
But a rainbow divine.

The Battle Of Blossoms And Light

Another mile, half a mile,
Sneeze a mile onward,
All to the valley of canals, of death.
"Achoo!, venture forward!
Charge for the fields!" We said.
Into the valley of canals, of death.

Is there a nose left unencumbered?
Not though the wonderer beholds
No fear
No reason
No remorse
Just a tear, or a drizzle, or a dizzy spell.
Into the valley of canals, of death.

Pollen under footing,
Pollen from the skies,
Pollen in the winds
Smashed and berated;
Caught in a life-giving spell.
Fervently on,
Like hell in their noses,
Into the valley of canals, of death.

O how we kneel to natures relent,
Ode to the fields of relentless.
Always, a person shall return calloused,
In the battle of blossoms and light.

Valley Of Eden

As I walk, as I walk,
As I walk through a valley of Eden,
Of softest warmth,
Of an effervescent glow,
Of a flower's iridescent embrace.
Beauty's smile o'er the pastures,
Of brisk winds,
Alas, from the besom of angels,
That hold,
That humble.

As I walk, as I walk,
As I walk high the valley of Eden,
Of a dawn invite to a wondrous place.
The heart in the valley, and Eden's embrace.

Echoes Of Colour

Life sails at dawn,
Echoes of colour flood sky.
Far, far beyond I.

Bloom's Embrace

Growing, growing,
Rebirth's arms reach;
With open arms, they kiss the throws of dawn.
A light that echoes beyond, eternal.
A grasp for the milk of horizon,
Of morning's dew,
Of an emanating storm that rejoices.
That rejoices and dances,
And breathes life in a blanket of nether.
No prejudice.
No illusion.

The sun and the moon smile upon,
As they watch the life, create.
The sun, the moon, the stars, and the light,
In the wake of a bloom's embrace.

Spring City Life

The streets were singing in angelic flight.
The neon, in the quake of the cold.
Ripples of time are lost in the rain,
And fall in the silence,
And fall in the darkest dark and night.

The winds still bitter the bravest man,
The warmth is still in hiding.
Envious are the flakes of the fall,
For now, new life is calling.

Nature's Call

Nature calls. Frost weeps.
Dreams from over the rainbow.
Flowers, streams, give life.

Your Song In April

Did I reach you in the longing nights?
Did I reach you in the rain?
Did I reach you on the precipice,
That stared the stars with most ethereal of mane?

Did I reach you?
Can I reach you?
Will I reach you on the warmest plight,
Of heart's might, of earnest?

Did I reach you on the mountains?
Did you hear me in the sands?
As I held you in the purest waters,
Did you hear me in the diamond light?

Did you hear me from the heavens?
Did you hear the song from the skies?
Did I reach you in the looking glass,
Through a window pane, through all sight?

Pray the Gods smite it all for the farthest star,
To gift, to find. To give it all.
So you can hear the song of April's night,
The song of harmony.
The song of will and delight.

Clear Blue

Winds breathe, eternal,
Wipes away the snow tears.
Blue skies lost in rain.

Hello. Goodbye.

Inside the waters,
Rebirth now begins to grow.
Life brings, takes. Hello.

Dew Forms

Let it be fallen,
My child of the crescent skies.
Form on sombre haze.

Busy Bee

Flee, like a message
Lost in the tides of a wind.
Bees hustle; life now crows.

Grey Gardens

The jungle sleeps as the lions roar,
Like bones entrenched,
Like stones in the belly of a beast.

The jungle weeps for a shackled strand,
Of pollen,
Of substance,
Of a manacle, weakened by augmenting sun.

The jungle sleeps as the lions roar,
But now the greys
But now they submit, surrender,
To dye in the hue of green and rose.

The jungle sleeps.
The jungle grows and sleeps.

Deiformis

Were you the world's kneaded bread,
Embroidered with starlight, and heavenly scent,
Incrusted with the sugar of water's sweet bed,
I'd fly beyond angels, with the birds and the bees.
I'd soar with the bats, and the owls within trees.
I'd be of all colours, with a tinge of the sky,
And succulent fruits, deiform and divine:
But you're just a leaf, and I am the larval,
I'll still be the butterfly an eye will still marvel,
But a red or a purple,
A blue or a green.
I, just a caterpillar, on a bed of life's green.
I, just a caterpillar, that remains to be seen.

The Song Of All Seasons

"Goodnight," waved the tadpole.
"Sleep well," chirped the robin,
The heat will ascend, forests, foxes, and trees.

The seas were now restful,
The beaches had breeze,
But all along coastlines the tides of all tease.

Gone be the frozen,
Lost was the rain.
In the song of all seasons, we will hear it again.
In the song of all seasons, it was spring once again.

Stephen M. Forrester (born December, 1983), is a British musician with a successful career in the aerospace industry. His muse is his partner, nature is his guide, and when he is not busy, he is found lost in fantasy adventures and the Wiltshire countryside.

Influenced by greats such as Yeats and Tennyson, Stephen's work is an expression of love and life that recaptures the essence of the golden eras, and revives them for a modern world.

www.stephenmforrester.com

Printed in Great Britain
by Amazon